T0197456

Crystal's Insight

Crystal Chantell Ned

To order additional copies of this book, contact:
Xlibris
844-714-8691
www.Xlibris.com
Orders@Xlibris.com

ISBN: Softcover   978-1-4500-5567-3

Library of Congress Control Number: 2010902996

Print information available on the last page

Rev. date: 04/22/2024

Contents

My Life

My life has been filled with trials and tribulations

I've had hills to climb

But through it all I kept God by my side

I've been hurt, lied on, and mistreated

God has seen me through it all

For I know for certain now

That God sees me through all my endeavors

God fights all my battles

And he makes my enemies my footstool

For God says No Weapon Formed Against Me Shall Prosper

I claim through Christ Jesus who strengthens me

A long happy prosperous life

Change Me Lord

Lord mold me and make me into what you want me to be

Change my mind,and thoughts to reflect solely on you

Lord give me the strength, courage and knowledge I need

To continue on day by day in this troubled world

Lord give me the prayer you want me to pray each day

Lord give me the words you want me to say

Lord give me the lifestyle you want me to live

Lord with you as my all and all everything else falls into place

Lord Give Me Strength

Lord give me strength to continue on each day

To carry on doing your will

To live according to your will

To serve you in all I say and do

Give me strength to share your holy word

Give me strength to sing your holy praises

Lord lead me and guide me

That I may walk in your footsteps

Lord let me never walk alone

When I'm tried carry me

A Time For Change

There's a time for playing

There's a time for procrastinating

There's a time for unbelief

There's no time for fighting

There's no time for faking with God

There's no time for doubting God

There's no time trying to hurt others

For God sees all and knows all

It's time to be ready for God

For he's coming for each of us

Anointed One

For you are anointed by the blood of Jesus

Jesus chose you to speak his word

He anointed you from head to toe with his blood

Your anointed body is Jesus vessel

Your anointed lips shall speak his word

Your anointed hands shall bless his people

Have no fear for no harm can come onto you

For you are covered by the blood of Jesus

Enemies try to destroy

But no man can hender your blessings

They are blessings from Jesus

What Jesus gives you can't no man take it away

Dedicated To: Rev. Lonnie Guillory II

Covered By His Blood

Being covered by Jesus blood is truly a blessing

It protects my family and I from all hurt, harm, and danger

The blood of Jesus protects us from our enemies

We shall not fear for the wicked can't get near

The devil tries to approach us but he stumbles and fall

The devil can't steal our joy for it's given by Jesus

Any thing given by Jesus is well given

Have Faith

Seek and ye shall find

Claim it and it shall come to past

Believe it and you shall achieve it

Pray and your prayers shall be answered

Give it to God and leave it there

For what's in God's hands is in good hands

People With Power

People in leadreship feel they have power

Without the power of Jesus Christ

You have nothing

For the power of Jesus is truly

Blessed power that last indefinately

Power given by man only last a season

For man power is limited and at times wicked

Jesus power has no limitations and no fear

Woman of God

Your kind words you say to all

Your unselfish thoughts you portray

Your caring outreach to all

Your loving and motherly ways

Your thoughtful prayers you send up above

Your prayerful lifestyle you lead

Your Godly light shines through and through

Be Aware

Be aware of wolf in sheep clothing

For they are not of God they are pretenders

God will make his people aware of those whom aren't of him

God will protect his people from the unrighteous and evil

For God will fight all our battles and win

God is the almighty father and he will take care of all his people

God see all and knows all, he knows those that aren't of him

God is such an awesome God that he loves those against him

Let's model our life after God and love those against us

Family

Family are often consisted of blood relatives

People genetically attached to you

People bonded by marriage

To me family is people whom you connect with on many levels

Family are people who truly care for you

Family are people whom help you in your time of need

Family are people who are willing to give you their last

Family are kind, gentle, caring, forgiving people we cherish

Jerrett Life Is

Life is a gift from God

Life is too precious to take for granted

Life on earth is fiiled with trials to endure

Battles to win and Hills to climb

Life on earth is not promised forever

Live life to it's fulliest

Live life according to God's will

Through God all things are possible

With God you can concure your trials

Win your battles and climb your hills

Know that through Christ that strengthens you

You can do all things

Life is what you make of it and not what man gives you

My Little Love

You are my heaven sent gift

You're my first and only child

You're truly a blessing to all you encounter

You have a gift from God

You're anointed by God

The devil tries but he can't get near you

You will be talked about, lied on, and mistreated

So was Jesus

Do know what Jesus has for you is for you

Be blessed in the Lord

For you are the little love of my life

Dedicated To: Jerrett Paul Ramagor

Love At First Sight

From the first time I looked into your eyes

I new you were the one

The one I want to spend my life with as one

Life throws us curve balls hard to caugh

But with God in our lifes

Nothing is too hard to achieve as one

Some people try to come between us

But when God is in the mist no one can intervene

Dedicated To: JC Jack

To my Love JC

JC my love I love you more than words can say

I love you more than gifts can show

I love you more than expressions can express

I love you more than some can believe

I love you during the happy and the sad

The good and the bad

My love has no limits

My love has no conditions

My love is real

My love is true

My love is and will always be here for you

Age Is Just A Number

Age is just a number

Man puts limitations on us according to our age

But God has no limitations on us regardless of our age

Young or old happiness is the key

God died for all our sins

We are all entitled to peace, happiness, and joy

It may take a young woman to bring happiness to an older man

Live and let live

Love and be loved

Happiness is for all to enjoy

JC Jack

Jesus touched and chosen one

Confident in the word of the lord

Jesus perfect creation

Angel sent from heaven

Caring to all

Knowledgeable of God's teachings

Not Too Far

Although I can't see you

I know you are here

Standing by my side looking over me

All so close to me you will always be

I will live by the godly ways you've taught me

I will always remember you

I had to let you go into the gates of glory

For God loved you more

I thank God for loaning you to me

My life was complete having you as my grandmother

Dedicated To: Juanita L. Ned

To My Sister

Through the good and the bad

The happy and the sad

We stood up for each other always

My little sister you have been and will always be in my heart

Through God that strengthens me I will be strong

I know that you're in a better place

My little sister we will meet in heaven

When God calls me home

Dedicated To: Shakinda Rachelle Ned

The Author's Family, Author Crystal Ned , Fiancé JC Jack and son Jerrett Ramagor

Printed in the United States
by Baker & Taylor Publisher Services